BUILDING JEWISH LIFE
Shabbat

by Joel Lurie Grishaver from draft by Debra Markovic

photographs by Jane Golub, Joel Lurie Grishaver and Alan Rowe
additional photographs by Jules Porter and Faige Kobre

Illustrations by David Bleicher

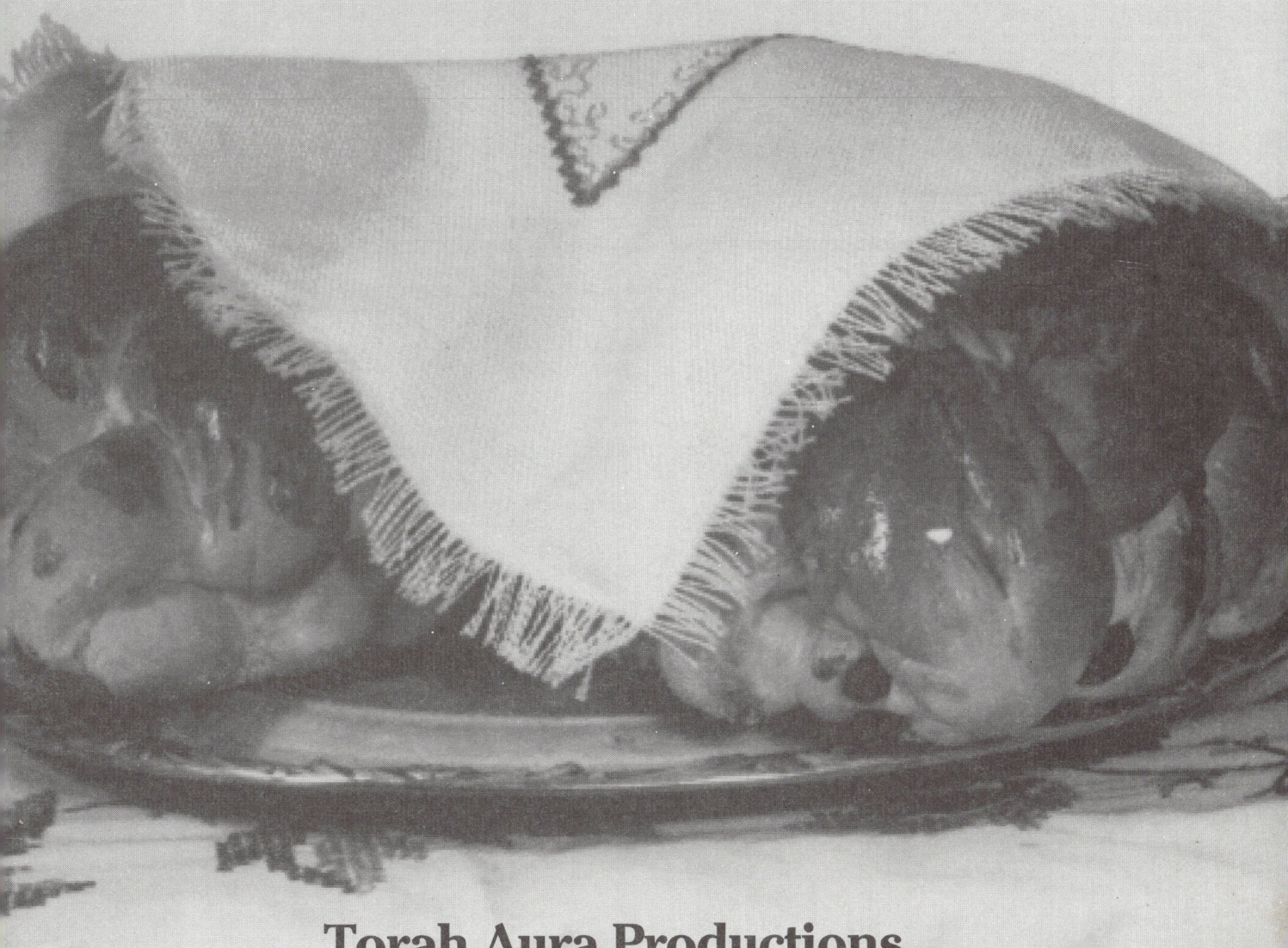

Torah Aura Productions
Los Angeles, California

For Joel Starin ז"ל.

Happy is the man who fears the Lord
*   who is ardently devoted to his commandments…*
All goes well with the man who lends generously
*   who conducts his affairs with equity…*
He gives freely to the poor
*   His beneficence lasts forever*
*   His horn is exalted forever.*
*   Psalm 112*

Thank You:
Ellen, Darrell, Zipper and Alexandra Lomas
Bernie, Kathleen, Michael and Amanda Borgeda
Temple Emanuel, Beverly Hills
Temple Beth El, San Pedro
Associated Talmud Torah, Chicago
Camp Ramah Family Camp, Ojai

Our Advisory Committee:
Melanie Berman, Yosi Gordon, Carolyn Starman-Hessel, Carolyn Moore-Mooso, Debi M. Rowe

Contributions
We gratefully acknowledge the kindness of the following for permission to use photographs from other works:
The Federation of Jewish Men's Clubs for photographs appearing on pages 1, 7, 14, 16, 17, 20, 22, 42, 43, and 44 taken from *The Art of Jewish Living: The Shabbat Seder,* © 1985.
Faige Kobre for photographs appearing on pages 6, 21, 23, 24, 41, 45, 46 from *A Sense of Shabbat*, Torah Aura Productions

Illustrations
All illustrations in this volume are ©1989 Dan Bleicher

ISBN# 0-933873-51-4
© 1990 Torah Aura Productions
All rights reserved. No part of this publication may be reproduced or transmitted in any form or by any means graphic, electronic or mechanical, including photocopying, recording or by any information strage and retrieval systems, without permission in writing from the publisher.

MANUFACTURED IN THE UNITED STATES OF AMERICA

TORAH AURA PRODUCTIONS
4423 FRUITLAND AVENUE, LOS ANGELES, CA 90058
(800) BE-TORAH • (800) 238-6724 • (323) 585-7312
FAX (323) 585-0327 • E-MAIL <MISRAD@TORAHAURA.COM
VISIT THE TORAH AURA WEBSITE AT WWW.TORAHAURA.COM

Part One: Preparing for Shabbat

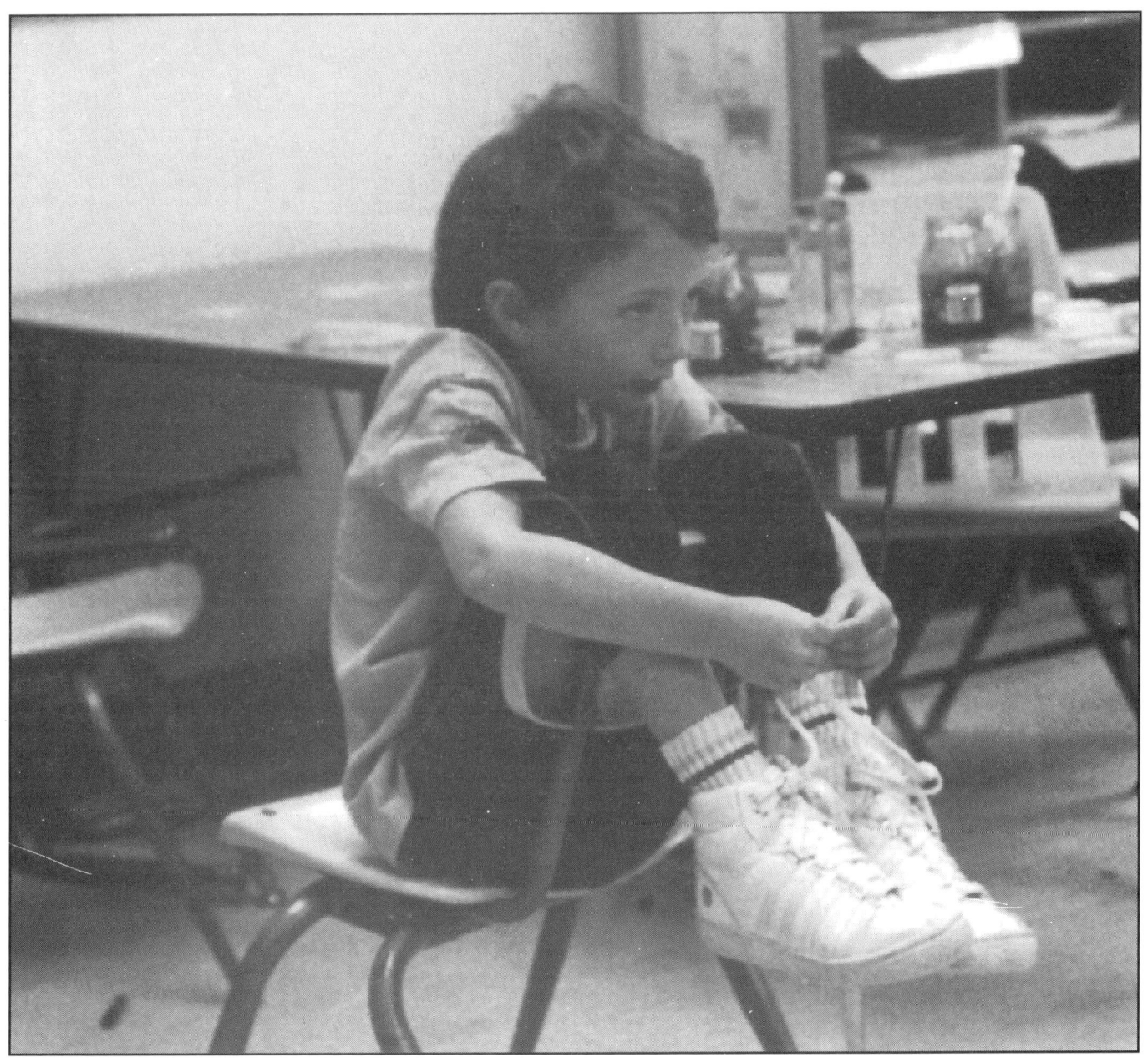

Think recess.

Five minutes before the bell rings, time starts moving faster than it has all morning. You finish your assignment. You straighten up your desk. You get your snack out of your backpack. You join the line that forms at the door. Even though recess comes every day, it is always exciting to get ready.

The bell rings, and instantly you are outside. The air smells crisp. Your snack tastes good. You run around the playground. Your whole body feels loose and free.

Recess is a time to talk. You get to tell your friends the things you have been saving up all day. Recess time is different. It looks, smells, tastes, sounds, and feels different. But, when recess ends, you go back to class.

RECREATION

Recess is a kind of recreation. Recreation has to do with fun, rest and play.

Re-creation is a way of becoming a new creation. After recess you feel renewed. You feel refreshed. It is as if you have been created anew.

Think Shabbat.

In many ways, Shabbat is a lot like recess. It too is recreation. It too is a way for us to become new creations.

Shabbat is a day set aside to play, rest, pray, and be with our families and friends. On Shabbat, we take a break from work and school.

Discussion:
How is Shabbat like recess?

On Shabbat, we remember that God created the universe in just six days. In the Torah we are told:

> The Families of Israel should guard the Shabbat.
> Jews of every age should make Shabbat,
> Forever, as an everlasting promise.
> Because in six days, God made the heavens and the earth,
> but on the seventh day, God made Shabbat and had recreation.
>
> *Exodus 31. 16–17*

We are commanded to follow God's example. It is a mitzvah for us to work for six days and then rest on Shabbat. Shabbat is when we take a recess from our regular work and become re-created.

Shabbat is something we make. Making Shabbat takes work, Shabbat takes preparation.

Discussion:
What does it mean to "make" Shabbat? How can you make a day?

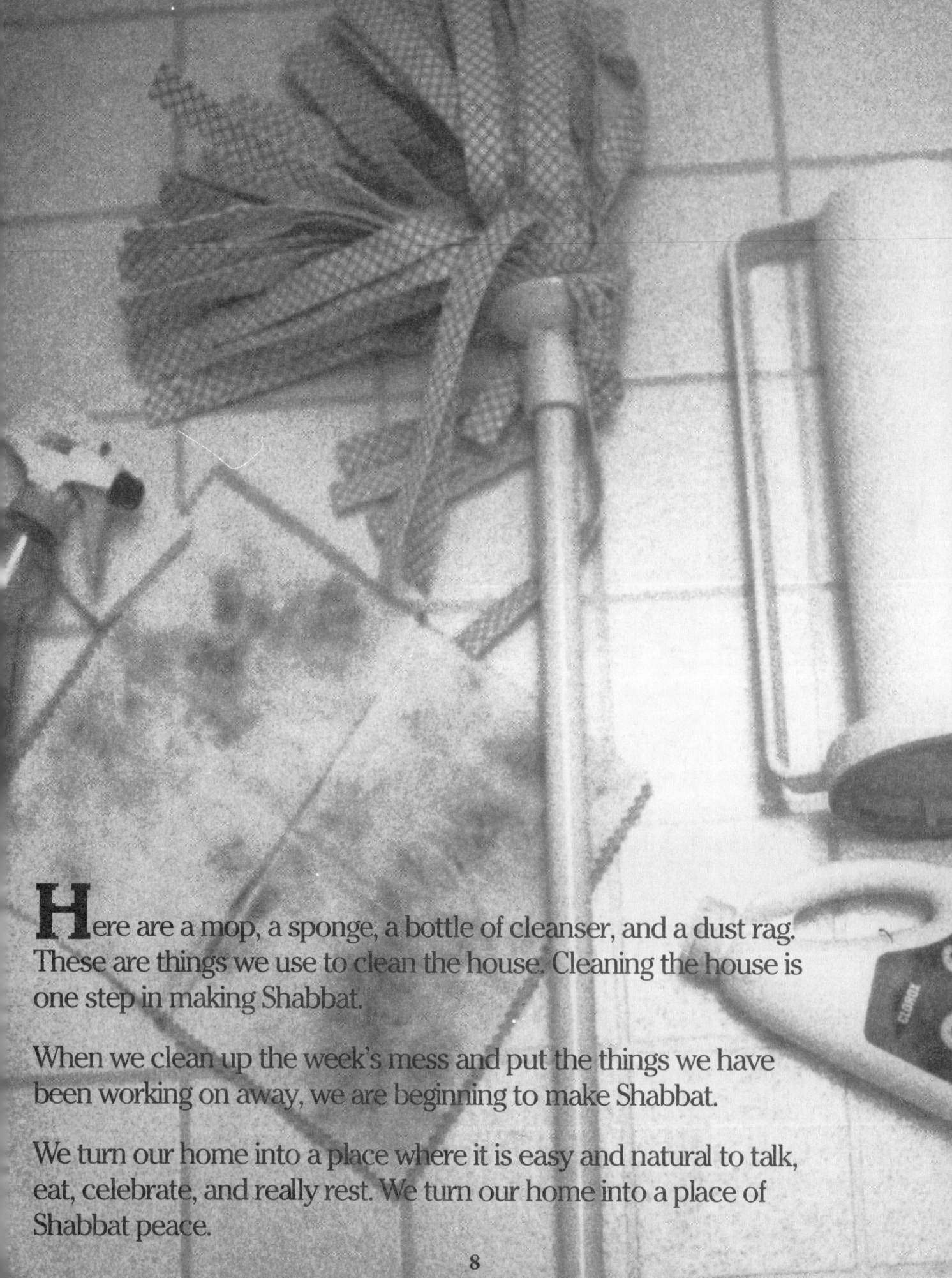

Here are a mop, a sponge, a bottle of cleanser, and a dust rag. These are things we use to clean the house. Cleaning the house is one step in making Shabbat.

When we clean up the week's mess and put the things we have been working on away, we are beginning to make Shabbat.

We turn our home into a place where it is easy and natural to talk, eat, celebrate, and really rest. We turn our home into a place of Shabbat peace.

Here are flour, a mixer, a bowl, a sifter, eggs, measuring cup, sesame seeds, a wooden spoon, raisins, and a baking pan. These are ingredients and utensils we use to make food for Shabbat. Cooking is another way we prepare for Shabbat.

The rabbis taught that a magic spice can creep into the food we make for Shabbat.

The Emperor, the Rabbi and a Spice Called Shabbat

Antoninus was a Roman Emperor. He had a good friend named Rabbi Yehuda ha-Nasi. One Shabbat, Rabbi Yehuda prepared lunch for his friend. The food was cold, because the Rabbi did not cook on Shabbat. Still, Antoninus pronounced everything "delicious."

"Mmmmm," said Rabbi Yehuda, raising his eyebrows like he knew a secret but couldn't tell.

Later that week, the Emperor again went to the Rabbi's house for dinner. This time, the Rabbi served him a piping hot meal. Antoninus tasted everything.

"This meat is okay," he said to the Rabbi, "and the vegtables aren't bad, but I enjoyed the last meal you made much more. This food is missing something."

©1989 DAVID BLEICHER

The Rabbi loved his friend and so he tried not to laugh.

"Well, something's missing," said the Emperor. "Did you forget something, or is it a secret recipe that has been handed down from one Jewish family to another, year after year after year? Come on, you can tell me. What is it?"

"Okay, my friend, you're right," replied Rabbi Yehuda. "Something is missing. But you won't find it in the pantry. You won't find it in the cellar either. You won't find it in the cabinet, in the rear or on top. You won't even find it in my box of 'secret recipes that have been handed down from one Jewish family to another for year after year after year.'

"What's missing," continued the Rabbi "is a spice that can't be grown, can't be mixed, can't be found or tasted anywhere. You see," he said, "what's really missing is not an ingredient at all, but the Shabbat itself."

Talmud Shabbat 119a

This is a **tzedakah box**. Giving tzedakah is the last way we prepare for Shabbat.

Tzedakah is the mitzvah of giving some of what we have to help other people who are in need. Just before we light the Shabbat candles and begin Shabbat, we put a few coins in the Tzedakah box. It helps us find our Shabbat spirit.

Isaiah was a prophet. He taught:

> Doing **tzedakah** will make **peace**,
> and the work of **tzedakah** will bring **calm** and **comfort**
> for all time."

32:17

Discussion:
How does giving tzedakah prepare us for Shabbat? How does it bring calm and comfort?.

This is a table. It is a place where we eat, talk, spend time as a family, and maybe even do homework.

This is a Shabbat table. It is an ordinary table which has been prepared for Shabbat. Here, we pray, talk, eat, study, sing, and become closer as a family.

On Shabbat we have a short service at the table before we eat dinner.

Discussion:
How does an ordinary table become a Shabbat table?

Part Two: Welcoming Shabbat

These are Shabbat candles. When we light them just before the sun sets on Friday evening, Shabbat begins.

Every Shabbat, Jews light at least two candles. When we bless these two flames, we learn two lessons about Shabbat. One flame teaches us about **"Remember,"** while the other teaches us about **"Guard."**

The two candles teach us that Shabbat retells two stories: the "Remember" story and the "Guard" story. To understand these stories we need to know about the Ten Commandments.

On top of Mt. Sinai, God taught Moses Ten Commandments. The fourth commandment was about Shabbat. In the Torah, we find the Ten Commandments in the book of Exodus and again in the book of Deuteronomy. The commandment about Shabbat is told one way in one book and a different way in the other.

In the book of Exodus, we are told to "**Remember** Shabbat and keep it holy." Here, the Torah explains that God created the world in six days and rested on the seventh. On Shabbat, we should follow God's example. One day a week we try not to make or control things. Instead, we live quietly. We take a rest.

In the book of Deuteronomy, we are told to "**Guard** Shabbat and keep it holy." Here, the Torah explains that when we were slaves in Egypt, God freed us. Only free people can choose to spend a day resting.

15

One candle teaches us that when we celebrate Shabbat we are like Adam and Eve having Shabbat in the Garden of Eden. When we look at the world on Shabbat, we can really see the wonders which God created. Shabbat is the one day when we stop trying to change creation. We do no work. Instead, we let the wonders of creation change us.

The other candle teaches us that when we celebrate Shabbat we are like Moses and the Families of Israel who celebrated Shabbat for forty years in the wilderness. We are free. We can choose when to work. We can choose not to work. When we celebrate Shabbat we celebrate our freedom.

*Discussion:
How can a candle teach a lesson?*

Shabbat is a good time to have guests. After the candles are lit, we gather around the table and sing **Shalom Aleikhem**. This Shabbat song welcomes guests. It also welcomes the Shabbat angels.

The Shabbat Angels

Two angels visit Jewish homes each Friday night. When they arrive at the house, they check to see if the Shabbat candles are lit, if the table is set, and if there is a sense of peace. They want to know whether Shabbat has been made.

If Shabbat has been made, the good angel says "May this family have a Shabbat like this every week!" and the evil angel is forced to say, "Amen."

But if Shabbat has not been made, the evil angel says "May this family have a Shabbat like this every week!" and the good angel is forced to say, "Amen."

Talmud Shabbat 119b

Discussion:
Are there really angels?

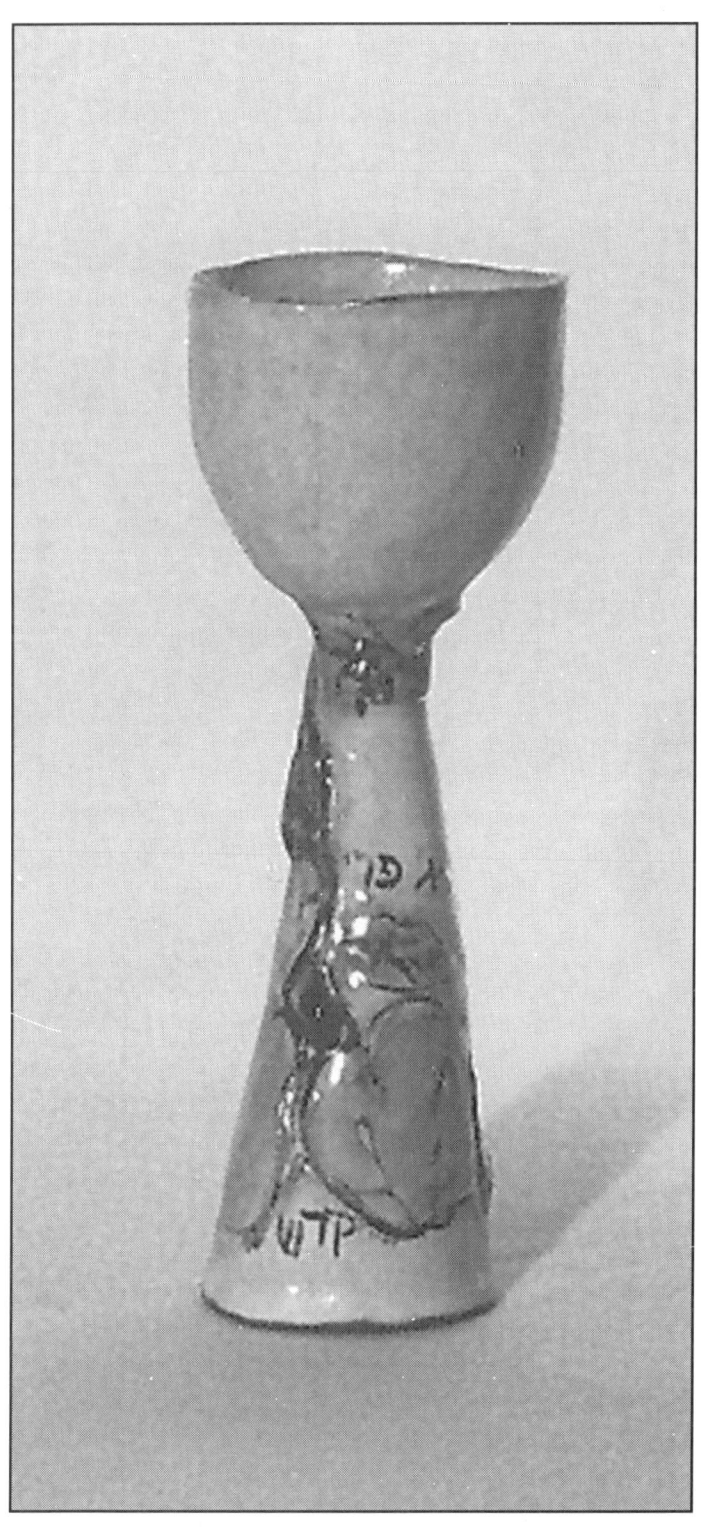

This is a **Kiddush cup**. It teaches us that a few words can change everything. "Kiddush" means "holy." It is the name of the brakhah said over a cup of wine on Shabbat and holidays.

When we say a few words over a cup of wine, Shabbat becomes a holy time. A few words change everything.

Even though Friday would be Shabbat even if we didn't light candles and say the Kiddush, the words of the Kiddush do make a difference. By saying a few words over a cup of wine, we make Shabbat our holy time.

*Discussion:
What makes a time holy time?*

A blessing is a wish. On Shabbat, parents ask God to bless their sons and daughters. With a hug, with a few words whispered in the ear, and with a kiss, they share their love as a hope for the future. Shabbat is a time to think about the future.

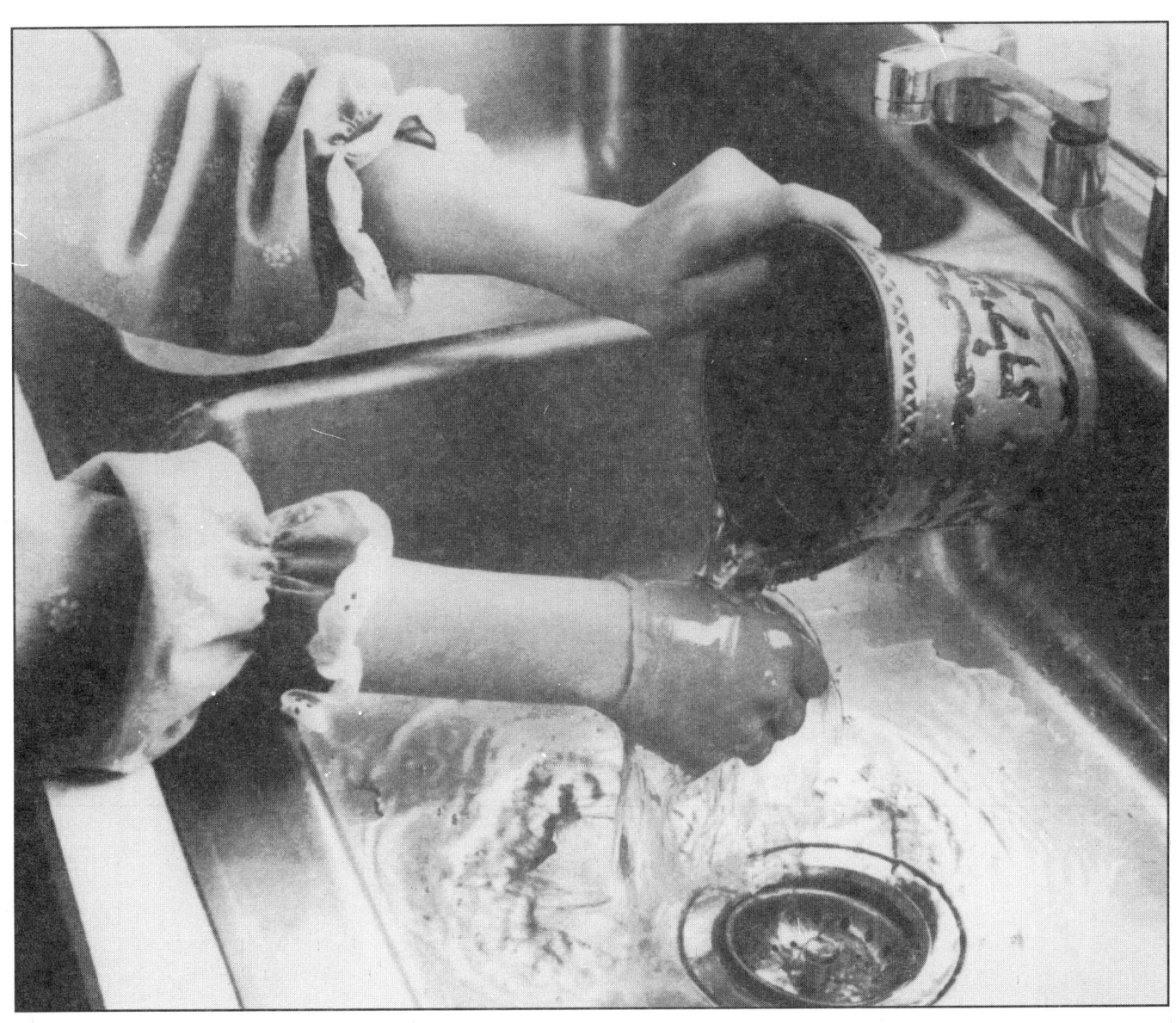

Something as simple as washing our hands can teach us a lesson. This special cup is used for *netilat yadayim*, the ceremony for washing hands. It teaches us a lesson.

Netilat yadayim means "lifting up hands." When we do this ritual before we eat, we pour water over each of our hands, lift them up in the air, and then say a brakhah. The lifting up teaches us that when we eat a meal together, it becomes a holy time. To get ready, we lift ourselves up.

Discussion:
Why is holiness something to which we "come up?"

These are **hallot**. A hallah is braided bread that often comes with raisins or sesame seeds or poppy seeds. It can be round or square, big or small. It is delicious! When we eat hallah on Shabbat, we remember that every day of the forty years when they wandered in the desert, God fed the Families of Israel with manna.

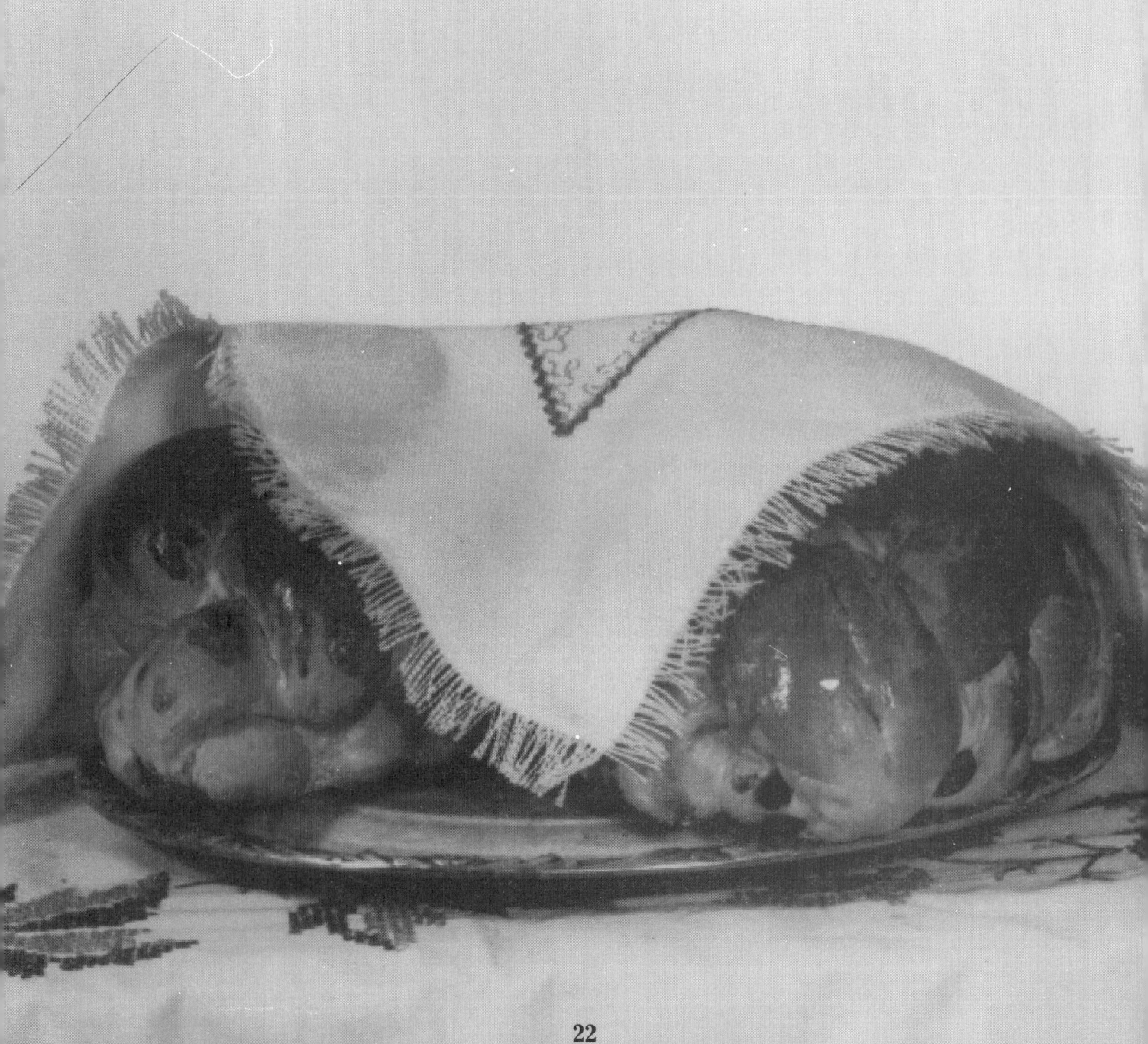

After the short service is finished, it is finally time to eat the outstanding Shabbat dinner which we worked so hard to make!

After we are done eating, we sit around the table for a while. There is nowhere to rush, nothing which must be done. We have time to be together.

Sometimes we sing Shabbat songs called *zemirot*. Sometimes we read or tell stories. Sometimes we just talk. There is a lot to talk about. A whole week has gone by.

This is a **benscher**. Benscher is the yiddish word for the booklet that contains **Birkat ha-Mazon**, the brakhah said after eating. Birkat ha-Mazon is the way that Jews fulfill the mitzvah found in the Torah:

> After you have eaten and become full
> You should bless Adonai, Your God.

Deuteronomy 8.10

Discussion:
Why is it important to say brakhot to thank God?

24

Part Three: Shabbat Day

Shabbat is a time when Jews gather in the synagogue.

In the synagogue, we pray and sing, we hear the Torah being read, and we spend time with our friends.

Shabbat is one time when families join together to become a community.

This is a family room. On Shabbat it becomes a place to get together with family and friends. We put our feet up, talk, perhaps play a game, or just spend time together.

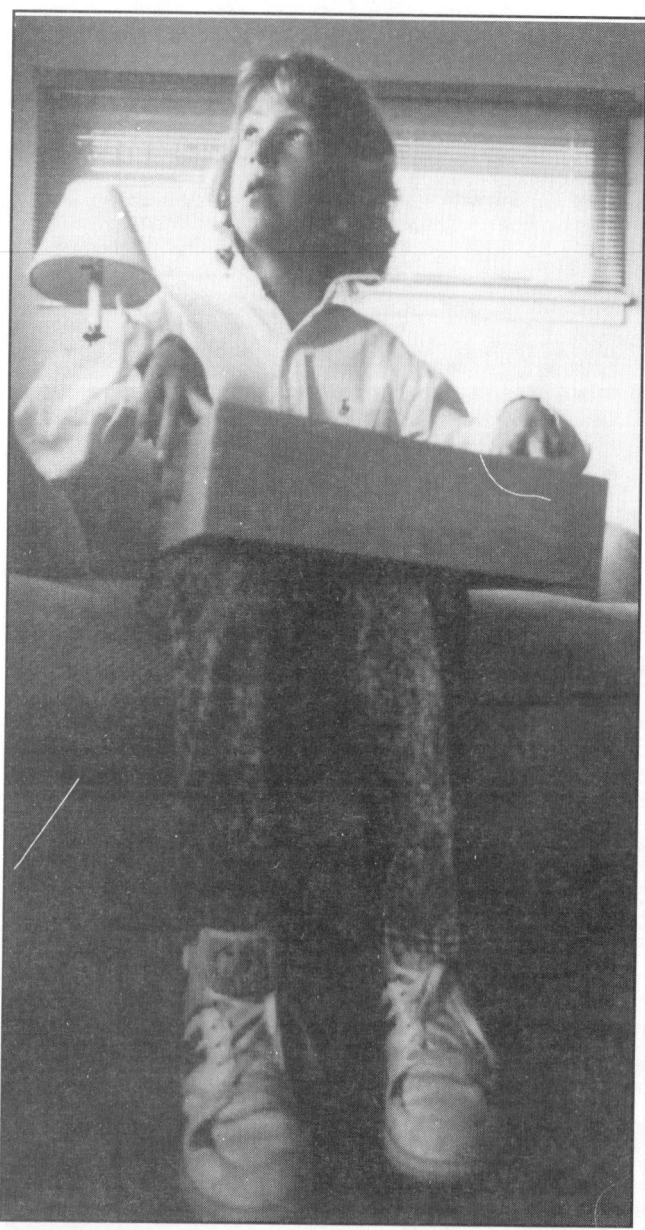

These are sneakers. They, too, can be an important part of Shabbat. Going on walks is a great Shabbat thing to do. Walking rather than riding lets us really see, smell, hear and touch things. It reminds us that God created the world and then rested.

This is a bookcase. Shabbat is also a great time to just lie around and read.

This is a couch. Napping is also a great Shabbat activity. Lots of adults can't make it through Shabbat without a nap.

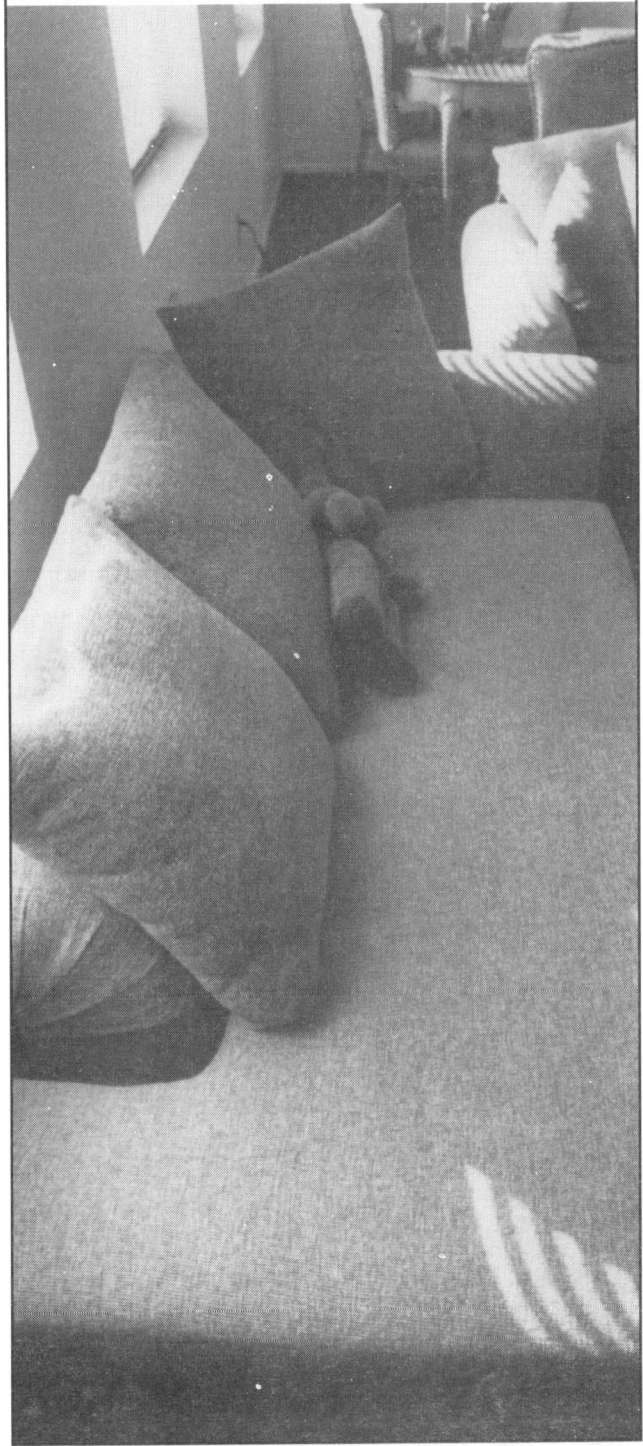

Part Four: Ending Shabbat

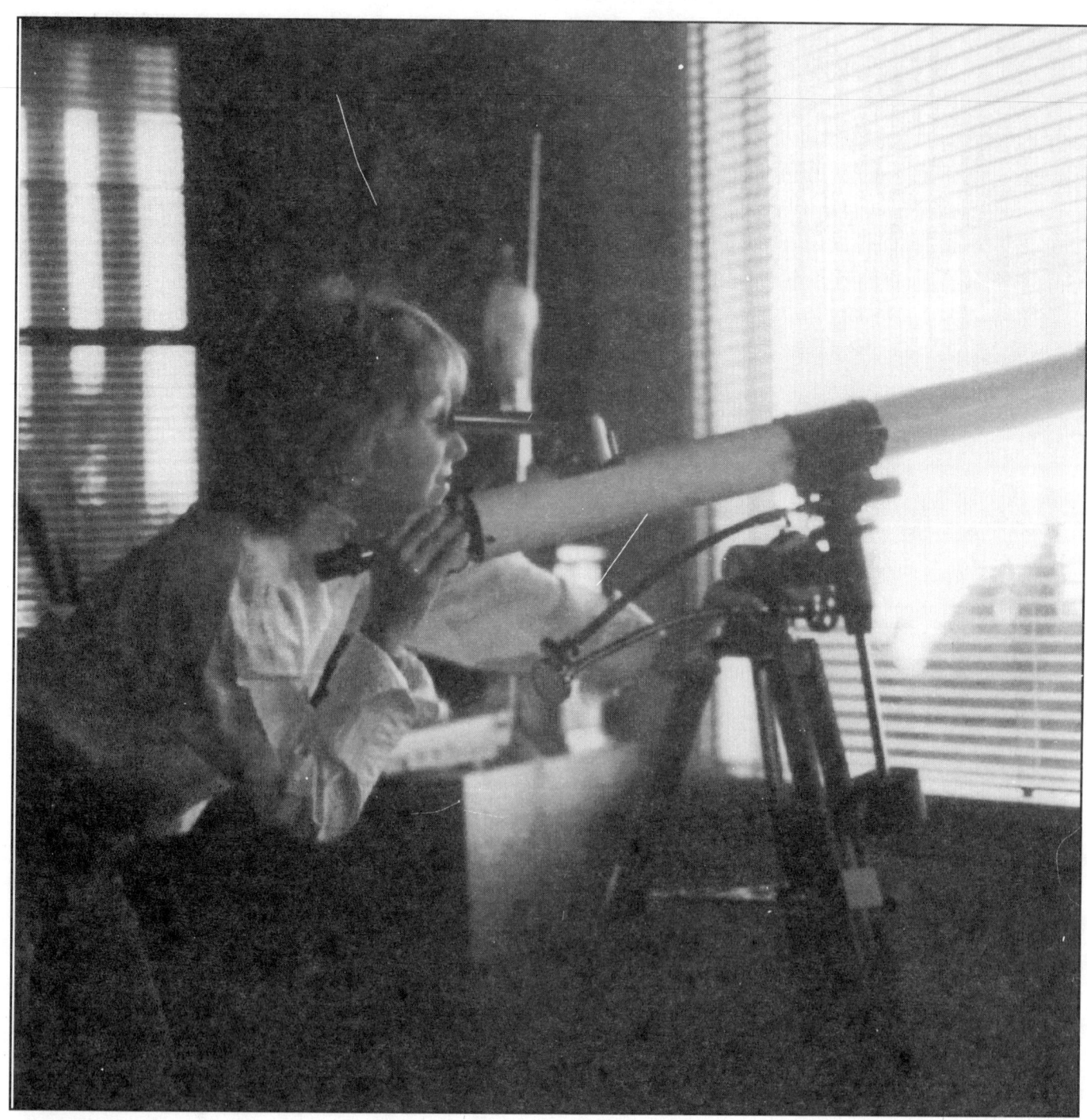

When we can see at least three stars, we know that it is really nighttime. We can end Shabbat any time after three stars can be counted.

Here are a **Kiddush cup**, a **Spice Box**, and a *Havdalah* **candle**. These three things are used to end Shabbat.

Havdalah means "division." The havdalah ceremony divides Shabbat from the week. It is a way of saying "good-bye" to Shabbat and the week that has passed. It is also a way of saying "hello" to the new week.

On Friday evening we begin Shabbat by lighting candles and saying kiddush. On Saturday night we end it in almost the same way.

When we bless the wine for havdalah, we fill the kiddush cup up to the very top. We even let some wine spill over. This reminds us that our hope is that the new week will be overflowing with happiness.

This is a **spice box.** It is filled with sweet-smelling things like cinammon or cloves. It, too, has a lesson to teach.

A smell is often easy to remember but very hard to describe. The rabbis taught that the special experiences we have on Shabbat are a lot like wonderful smells. Remembering the smell of the spice box helps us to gather together our special Shabbat moments.

*Discussion:
What are some of your special Shabbat memories?*

Havdalah candles are braided. They must have at least two wicks. The havdalah candle reminds us of all the connections we have made on Shabbat. It reminds us that as a family we are braided together.

The rabbis taught that someday the whole world would have Shabbat together. Someday, all people will live together in peace.

At the end of havdalah, after all the prayers our said, we put out the havdalah flame by dipping it into some of the wine. Then we usually sing a song about the prophet Elijah. Elijah will be the person who will announce the coming of the Great Shabbat when everyone will have peace.

Shabbat ends with the hope that someday Shabbat will never have to end.

Discussion:
What do you think the Great Shabbat will be like?

Ordering Shabbat

Pick the things which are done during the Table Service on Friday night. Number them 1, 2, 3, 4, 5, 6, and 7 to show their order.

Pick the things which are done during the Havdalah Service on Saturday night. Label them A, B, C, and D to show their order.

 ___Kiddush

 ___Wine

 ___Making the Division

 ___Spices

 ___Birkat Ha-Mazon

 ___Fire

 ___Blessing Children

 ___Shalom Aleikhem

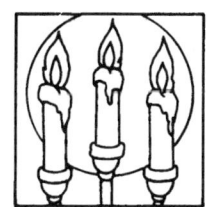 ___Lighting Candles

 ___Ha-Motzi

 ___Washing Hands

Home/The Shabbat Seder

Parents should reread pages 14 through 23 with their children. Then they should help them to imagine what each object would say. Finally, parents should write down the answers they create.

Image that the objects on the Shabbat table could talk. Think of the lesson that each would teach. Complete their lessons.

Candles

There are two of us. Together, we teach that Shabbat:

_____

_____

_____

Wine

When you say words over me, I make a magical change—I become holy. I can teach you that:

_____

_____

_____

Hallot

When you uncover us, we tell a story. We remind you that during the forty years in the wilderness:

_____

_____

_____

How to Bake Hallah

Things You Will Need:
   1/2 cup oil
   4 teaspoons salt
   3/4 cup sugar
   1 cup boiling water
   1/2 cup cold water
   2 packages dry yeast
   1/3 cup warm water
   3 eggs
   7-8 cups flour
   1/2 cup raisins (if desired)
   1 egg for topping
   Sesame or poppy seeds for topping

What to Do:
1. Pour the oil, salt and sugar into a large mixing bowl. Add 1 cup of boiling water. Stir. Add 1/2 cup of cold water. Stir.
2. Dissolve 2 packages of dry yeast in 1/3 cup warm water.
3. Beat 3 eggs and add to the oil mixture. Stir.
4. Add the dissolved yeast to the oil mixture. Stir.
5. Add 7 cups of flour, one cup at a time. Stir well. If the batter looks sticky, add 1/4 to 1/2 additional cups of flour.
6. Turn the dough out onto a floured board. Knead for 10 minutes.
7. Spread oil onto the sides of a large bowl. Put the dough into the bowl and turn it over to coat the dough with the oil. Cover the bowl with a dish towel and place in a warm spot. Let the dough rise 1 and 1/2 hours.
8. Punch down the dough. Turn out onto a floured board and gently knead for about 1 minute. Knead in the raisins if desired.
9. Divide the dough into 3 pieces. Roll each piece in your hands to make a long strand of dough. Braid the 3 strands as you would braid hair, and turn under the edges.
10. Cover the hallah with a towel and let rise another 45 minutes.
11. Preheat the oven to 375°.
12. Beat the remaining egg and brush the top of the hallah. Sprinkle with poppy or sesame seeds if desired.
13. Bake for 50 minutes or until brown on top.

How to Make a Spice Box

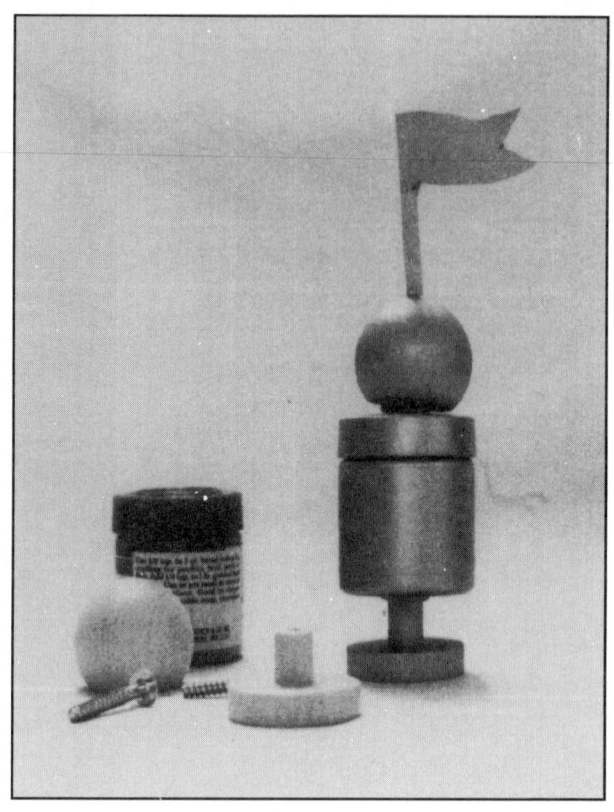

Things You Will Need:
- 1 small plastic jar of whole cloves
- 2 drawer knobs (from a hardware store)
- 1 piece of a wire coat hanger
- 1 piece of a plastic jug
- 2 screws
- Silver spray paint

Tools You Will Need:
- Drill with a very small bit
- Pliers
- Screwdriver
- Scissors
- Knife

What to Do:
1. Empty the cloves out of the jar and remove the plastic cover.
2. Cut a flag out of the plastic from the jug. Cut two small holes in it.
3. Cut a four-inch piece of coat hanger. Place the flag on the coat hanger.
4. Drill a small hole in the top of the round drawer knob and one in the plastic top of the spice jar. Then use the screw to attach the door knob to the plastic top from the spice jar. Finally, place the coat hanger in the hole in the top.
5. Drill a hole in the center of the bottom of the jar. Attach the second drawer knob to the bottom with the second screw.
6. Place the cloves back inside the jar. Replace the top. Spray paint silver. Allow to dry.

In the Talmud it says: "A person who says something in the name of the person who originally said it makes the world a better place " (Ta'anit 15b). We first saw this spice box at the second CAJE conference in Rochester, New York, in 1976. It was brought there by Cherie Koller-Fox. She learned it from Martin and Joan Farren.

FOR THE PARENT
BUILDING JEWISH LIFE

A PARTNERSHIP

This Building Jewish Life curriculum was designed in the belief that the best possible Jewish education happens only when the classroom and the home are linked. These pages are designed to cycle back and forth between those two realms, and to be used as a tool for learning in each. For this material to work most effectively, teacher and parent must assume interlocking roles and share in actualizing Jewish values and expressions. Each will do it in his/her own way. Each will do it with his/her own style. Together, they will reinforce each other, offering the child tangible experience and understanding of a visionary tradition.

MITZVAH CENTERED

Mitzvot is a word which means "commanded actions" and is used to describe a series of behaviors which Jewish tradition considers obligations. Classical Judaism teaches that the fabric of Jewish life is woven of 613 of these mandated actions. This series is built around the mitzvot, but it uses the term somewhat differently. In our day and age, the *authority* behind any "command" or obligation is a matter of personal faith and understanding. Each Jew makes his/her own peace or compromise with the tradition, affording it a place in his/her own life. In our age, the mitzvot have become rich opportunities. They are the things which Jews do, the activities by which we bring to life the ethics, insights, and wisdom of our Jewish heritage. Such acts as blessing holiday candles, visiting the sick, making a seder, comforting mourners, feeding the hungry, hearing the Purim *megillah*, studying Torah, educating our children, and fasting on Yom Kippur are all part of the *mitzvah*—Jewish behavior—"opportunity" list. They are actions which, when they engage us, create moments of celebration, insight, and significance. It is through the mitzvot that the richness of the Jewish experience makes itself available. Without addressing the "authority" behind the mitzvot, and without assuming "obligation," this series will expose the power of many *mitzvah*-actions and advocate their performance based on the benefit they can bring to your family. It does so comfortably, because we know that you will explore this material and make decisions which are meaningful for you and your family.

THE CLASSROOM

In the classroom, this volume serves as a textbook. It helps the teacher introduce important objects, practices, personalities and places in Jewish life. It serves as a resource for exploring Jewish values and engages the students in "making meaning" from Jewish sources. The inclusion of both a parent's guide and a teacher's guide at the end of this volume was an intentional act. We felt it was important for parents to fully understand what was being taught in the classroom.

THE HOME

This material suggests three different levels of home involvement. On the simplest level, it contains a number of parent-child activities which demand your participation. They cannot be completed without your help. None of these are information-centered. The task of teaching names, pronunciations and facts has been left for the classroom. Rather, these are all moments of sharing values and insights or experimenting with the application of that which has been learned in class. They should be wonderful experiences and they call upon you to be a parent interested in his/her child, not a skilled teacher or tutor.

On a second level, much of this material can also be used to provide "read-aloud" experiences at bedtime, or as the basis for family study and discussion at the dinner table. Do not be afraid to "pre-empt" that which will be taught in class, or to "review" that which your child has learned. The more reinforcement, the better.

Finally, and most dramatically, there is the experience of participating in the mitzvot described in this book. We strongly urge you to make this a year to "try out" as many of them as possible. Think of them as the field trips and home experiments which will enrich the classroom experience and make it comprehensible.

THE NETWORK

The prime focus of this text series is celebration. Celebrations are better when they are shared with friends. New activities and new challenges are easier when they are shared. Familiar activities are also enriched by the presence of others. Many of the congregations which adopt this series will already have a system of Havurot, Jewish Holiday Workshops, or family activities. Others will organize parallel parent education sessions and special events for the families of the students in this program. We also imagine that some families will network with their friends to "try out" some of these mitzvah-events. It is our strong suggestion that, at least on an event-to-event basis, you connect with other Jewish families to experience some of the celebrations about which your child will be learning.

Shabbat

Shabbat makes a difference!

One entire tractate of the Talmud is called *Eruvin*. According to traditional Jewish practice, on Shabbat, a person is not allowed to carry objects from an inside area to an outside area, or vice versa. The *Eruv* is a Shabbat boundary which makes everything within it one large "inside area" and which then excludes everything else.

In many ways the *Eruv* is a perfect metaphor for Shabbat itself. Most Jewish holidays make limited demands, they only take up a day or two of time (a week at most). Shabbat is different; it makes a regular demand. It wants its time slot each week. It sets up a boundary, leaving many things outside and unreachable (because you can't be home for Shabbat dinner with the family and attend the Winter Carnival Dance at the same time). Yet Shabbat also creates an inside—a regular opportunity for intimacy and connection—a protected moment for family and community.

The Keeper

Shabbat makes a difference. Perhaps more than any other Jewish opportunity, Shabbat makes a difference. A recent sociological study has confirmed what Ahad Ha-Am suggested almost a hundred years ago, "Even more than Israel has kept Shabbat, so Shabbat has kept Israel." So, too, this recent examination of the contemporary Jewish family has shown that the best predictor of adult Jewish identificaction is childhood participation in a family which "makes" Shabbat. This suggests something that Jewish educators have long known—Jewish education only makes a difference when it complements and enriches a home which enacts Judaism. Simply put, without any embellishment: Aall the efforts you put into providing your child with a Jewish education (and any actual impact you anticipate from his or her Jewish schooling) can best be insured by the creation of a regular home Shabbat experience.

Our purpose in this very brief parent's guide is three-fold. First, we want to affirm that if you are a family which has already evolved its own regular sense of Shabbat, it will most probably make a major difference. Second, if you are a family who is considering the development (or expansion) of a Shabbat experience, we want you to know that there is great advantage in doing so. And, third, we want to provide you with a set of resources to enable the continual growth of your family Shabbat experience.

Leisure Vs. Recreation

Jewish ideas grow slowly. Sometimes, when we follow them from their roots on, we learn a lot. Such is the case with Shabbat.

In the first chapter of the Torah we learn three things: God created the world. People were created in God's image. And, God worked for six days and then rested on the seventh. Later, when the Torah reflects on these things (and they come out as a commandment) all three ideas are combined. We are told (in Ex. 31.16-17): "*The Children of Israel shall KEEP Shabbat, they shall MAKE Shabbat, continually throughout their family histories, because in six days Adonai made heaven and earth, and on the Seventh Day God rested and was renewed.*"

The idea here is simple: First, because we are like God, we, too, have the right to rest on the Seventh Day (a lesson about *freedom* whose implications we will explore more in the next section). Second, and perhaps more importantly, the opposite is also true: By resting on the Seventh Day, we have the potental to become more like God. The key here, is the last word of this verse, *Va-Yinafash*, "renewal."

CLUB MED's marketing department understands the dynamics of *Va-Yinafash*; they know the difference between "leisure" and "recreation." **Leisure** is just "time available;" **recreation** is a process through which one's essence (the original creation) is "renewed." The word *Va-Yinafash* is rooted the Hebrew word *nefesh* which means "soul." A CLUB MED vacation is marketed as an opportunity to restore oneselves to one's essence. Shabbat was created as tool for perpetual self-renewal. The next time you wonder about the value of Shabbat, remember the beach in the CLUB MED ad.

For an individual, a real Shabbat, one which indeed breaks into the escalating stress and relentless pace of the workday week, is a major opportunity not only for self-restoration, but for personal growth. This is as true for children as it is for adults: A deep breath and a moment for reflection are valuable commodities. Shabbat offers both.

For families, whose lives are often guided by carpool routes that would confound an air traffic controller, whose convoluted set of commitments—usually displayed on the calendars hung on the refrigerator—would baffle a data processor, and whose constant expenditure of energy defy what most physicists teach about perpetual motion—Shabbat is a potential miracle. It would be trite to call it Judaism's organic "quality time." However, trite as it may be, it is appropriate. Shabbat is a calendared rest stop where the whole family is encouraged to pull over together and refresh themselves.

Shabbat is more than *leisure* time—it is a profound opportunity for *recreation*.

Take Two

The Ten Commandments appear twice in the Torah, once in the book of Exodus (when they are orginally given) and a second time in the book of Deuteronomy (where they are part of a historical retrospective). The two presentations are virutally identical except for the commandment about Shabbat. Whereas the Exodus version roots Shabbat in imitating God's rest, the Deuteronomy verson makes Shabbat an extension of the exodus from Egypt.

Simply put, Shabbat is *freedom*. Slaves can't choose their time to rest, a free people can. But, that is too simple. In truth, the lesson is deeper. Shabbat is a piece of our family history. The life changing moments in which lead a collection of slave families to risk their lives for a vision of the future is still part of who we are. As a Jewish family, we are the direct extension of moments of fleeing, crossing, standing, receiving, and accepting. (*If you need a key: a) Egypt, b) the Red Sea, c) At Mt. Sinai, d) the Torah, and e). the Torah*. Shabbat is at the core of that experience. We celebrate Shabbat because our families risked their lives to do so; and we celebrate Shabbat because it allows us to re-enter and re-experience the moments which tell us who were are.

The Shabbat of Exodus, the Shabbat of the Creation, is a per-

The idea here is simple: First, because we are like God, we, too, have the right to rest on the Seventh Day (a lesson about *freedom* whose implications we will explore more in the next section). Second, and perhaps more importantly, the opposite is also true: By resting on the Seventh Day, we have the potential to become more like God. The key here, is the last word of this verse, *Va-Yinafash*, "renewal."

CLUB MED's marketing department understands the dynamics of *Va-Yinafash*; they know the difference between "leisure" and "recreation." **Leisure** is just "time available;" **recreation** is a process through which one's essence (the original creation) is "renewed." The word *Va-Yinafash* is rooted the Hebrew word *nefesh* which means "soul." A CLUB MED vacation is marketed as an opportunity to restore oneselves to one's essence.

Shabbat was created as tool for perpetual self-renewal. The next time you wonder about the value of Shabbat, remember the beach in the CLUB MED ad.

For an individual, a real Shabbat, one which indeed breaks into the escalating stress and relentless pace of the workday week, is a major opportunity not only for self-restoration, but for personal growth. This is as true for children as it is for adults: A deep breath and a moment for reflection are valuable commodities. Shabbat offers both.

For families, whose lives are often guided by carpool routes that would confound an air traffic controller, whose convoluted set of commitments—usually displayed on the calendars hung on the refigerator—would baffle a data processor, and whose constant expenditure of energy defy what most physicists teach about perpetual motion—Shabbat is a potential miracle. It would be trite to call it Judaism's organic "quality time." However, trite as it may be, it is appropriate. Shabbat is a calendared rest stop where the whole family is encouraged to pull over together and refresh themselves.

Shabbat is more than *leisure* time—it is a profound opportunity for *recreation*.

Take Two

he Ten Commandments appear twice in the Torah, once in the book of Exodus (when they are orginally given) and a second time in the book of Deuteronomy (where they are part of a historical retrospective). The two presentations are virutally identical except for the commandment about Shabbat. Whereas the Exodus version roots Shabbat in imitating God's rest, the Deuteronomy verson makes Shabbat an extension of the exodus from Egypt.

Simply put, Shabbat is *freedom*. Slaves can't choose their time to rest, a free people can. But, that is too simple. In truth, the lesson is deeper. Shabbat is a piece of our family history. The life changing moments in which lead a collection of slave families to risk their lives for a vision of the future is still part of who we are. As a Jewish family, we are the direct extension of moments of fleeing, crossing, standing, receiving, and accepting. (*If you need a key: a) Egypt, b) the Red Sea, c) At Mt. Sinai, d) the Torah, and e). the Torah.* Shabbat is at the core of that experience. We celebrate Shabbat because our families risked their lives to do so; and we celebrate Shabbat because it allows us to re-enter and re-experience the moments which tell us who were are.

The Shabbat of Exodus, the Shabbat of the Creation, is a personal experience in which we, individually and as a family, search in quiet for our own essences, for the nature of creation. **The Shabbat of Deuteronomy**, the Shabbat of the Exodus from Egypt, is a communal experience, underlining our bonds with other Jewish families, past, present, and part of our vision of the future.

This twofold experience of Shabbat is continually reflected in our Shabbat practice: two candles, two *hallot*, the words of the Shabbat Kiddush, etc. all reflect this twofold understanding of how the celebration of one day a week can profoundly inform our values.

A Non-Constructivist Shabbat

raditionally, particularly in the language of Jewish practice, Shabbat was "made" through things one did not do. Shabbat was created through not working, not lighting fires, not doing business, etc. Out of these "do not" commandments, the rabbis of the Talmud created a positive whole. Quickly, let's follow their sleight of hand.

> *"Even more than Israel has kept Shabbat, so Shabbat has kept Israel."*

39

For The Teacher

The Shabbat volume of **Building Jewish Life** centers on three objectives:

1. Students will master the basic vocabulary of the celebration of Shabbat, consisting of words listed in the Essential Vocabulary section below.

2. Students will be able to explain the purpose of Shabbat as re-creation to their parents.

3. Students will be able to explain and participate in the preparation for Shabbat; giving tzedakah; welcoming Shabbat with candles, wine, and hallah and their blessings; washing hands; Birkat Ha-Mazon; and the Havdalah service.

ESSENTIAL VOCABULARY

Shabbat	the day of rest
Mitzvah	commandment
Tzedakah	sharing what we have with those in need
Hallah	braided loaf of bread for Shabbat
Kiddush Cup Shabbat	cup used specifically for blessing wine on
Netilat Yadayim	"lifting up hands", ritual hand washing.
Benscher	booklet containing *Birkat ha-Mazon*, grace after meals
Havdalah	"Separation", the ceremony that ends Shabbat
Spice box	Box filled with sweet spices

ADDITIONAL VOCABULARY

Candles
Wine
Shalom Aleikhem
Brakhah
Zmirot
Torah

LESSON ONE

1. SET INDUCTION: ASK "What do you know about Shabbat?" and list the students' answers on the blackboard. SAY "Believe it or not, we're going to begin learning about Shabbat by talking about recess." READ pages 3-7 in this book.

2. PREPARING FOR SHABBAT: DISCUSS "What does it mean to "make" Shabbat? How can you make a day?" Read pages 8-14.

3. MAKING HALLOT: READ page 22 in class. TELL the students that each of them will make hallot for their families to use on Shabbat. Have each student make a hallah in class. It might be nice to invite parents or grandparents to come in and help. Use the recipe on page 35.

LESSON TWO

1. SET INDUCTION: BRING candles in candlesticks, a kiddush cup, and two hallot. Hold them up. Explain their names. Let the students touch/taste them. SAY: "Let's take a look at how we use these things to help us taste and feel the "spice of Shabbat." READ pages 14-22.

2. DEMONSTRATE THE EREV SHABBAT TABLE SERVICE: USE the ritual objects brought to the class session and demonstrate the service.

3. TEXT READING: READ in class the prayers found on pages 41-46. DISCUSS why we are thanking God, and how these brakhot help us to do that.

4. MAKING SHABBAT: MAKE kiddush cups, candle holders, or other ritual items or decorations. **Fast, Clean and Cheap**, by Simon Kops, has some wonderful ideas that are easy and fun. If your school doesn't have a copy, call us at 1-800-BE TORAH and we'll send you one.

LESSON THREE

1. SET INDUCTION: BRING Havdalah candle, a kiddush cup, and a spice box. Hold them up. Explain their names. Let the students touch/taste/smell them. SAY: "Let's take a look at how we use these things to help us to say goodbye to Shabbat." READ pages 28-32.

2. DEMONSTRATE THE HAVDALAH SERVICE: USE the ritual objects brought to the class session and demonstrate the service.

3. TEXT READING: READ in class the prayers found on pages 47-48. DISCUSS why we are marking the division between Shabbat and the week to come, and how these brakhot help us to do that.

4. MAKING HAVDALAH: MAKE spice boxes, kiddush cups, or braided Havdalah candles. Instructions for making spice boxes are on page 36.

LESSON FOUR

Shabbat is the quintessential family holiday. This unit should culminate in bringing the students' families together. Hold a Shabbat dinner shared by the families of all the students in the class. Invite them all to the synagogue or to one family's home for a pot luck dinner. The students can use the ritual objects and decorations they have made—and all should help to prepare the room for Shabbat. Of course their hallot should be served, and the students should lead this large family in the Erev Shabbat table service, zmirot and Birkat Hamazon.

Friday Night Table Service

1
Tzedakah

It is a custom to begin Shabbat by putting a few coins in a Tzedakah box.

2
Candle Lighting

1. Light candles first.
2. Circle flames with hands one to three times. Finish by covering your eyes.
3. Recite the blessing.
4. Uncover eyes.
5. Hug and kiss—wish each other "Shabbat Shalom."

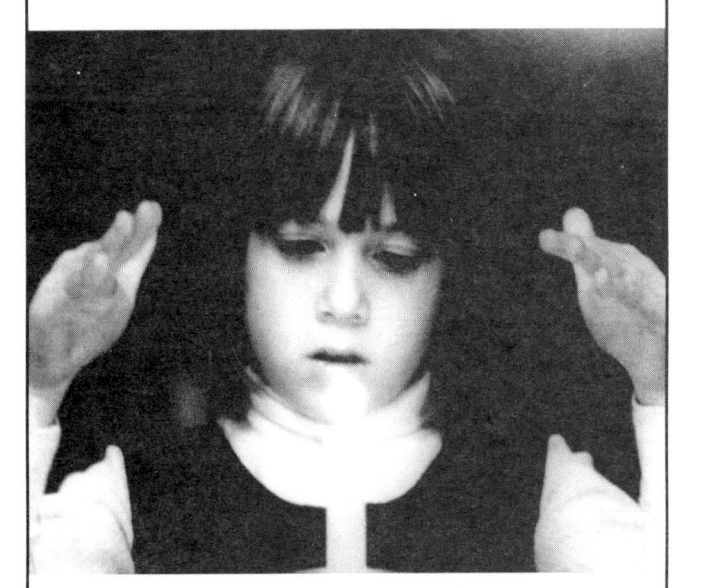

בָּרוּךְ אַתָּה יהוה
אֱלֹהֵינוּ מֶלֶךְ הָעוֹלָם
אֲשֶׁר קִדְּשָׁנוּ בְּמִצְוֹתָיו
וְצִוָּנוּ לְהַדְלִיק נֵר שֶׁל שַׁבָּת.

Barukh atah Adonai
Eloheinu melekh ha-olam
asher kidshanu b'mitzvotav
v'tzivanu l'hadlik ner shel Shabbat.

Praised are You, Adonai, our God, Ruler of the Cosmos, who made us holy through the mitzvot and made it a mitzvah for us to kindle the Shabbat lights.

3
Shalom Aleikhem

שָׁלוֹם עֲלֵיכֶם
מַלְאֲכֵי הַשָּׁרֵת
מַלְאֲכֵי עֶלְיוֹן
מִמֶּלֶךְ מַלְכֵי הַמְּלָכִים
הַקָּדוֹשׁ בָּרוּךְ הוּא.

בּוֹאֲכֶם לְשָׁלוֹם
מַלְאֲכֵי הַשָּׁלוֹם
מַלְאֲכֵי עֶלְיוֹן
מִמֶּלֶךְ מַלְכֵי הַמְּלָכִים
הַקָּדוֹשׁ בָּרוּךְ הוּא.

בָּרְכוּנִי לְשָׁלוֹם
מַלְאֲכֵי הַשָּׁלוֹם
מַלְאֲכֵי עֶלְיוֹן
מִמֶּלֶךְ מַלְכֵי הַמְּלָכִים
הַקָּדוֹשׁ בָּרוּךְ הוּא.

צֵאתְכֶם לְשָׁלוֹם
מַלְאֲכֵי הַשָּׁלוֹם
מַלְאֲכֵי עֶלְיוֹן
מִמֶּלֶךְ מַלְכֵי הַמְּלָכִים
הַקָּדוֹשׁ בָּרוּךְ הוּא.

Shalom aleikhem malakhei
ha-shareit malakhei Elyon
mi-Melekh Malkhei
ha-Melakhim
Ha-Kadosh barukh Hu.

Bo'akhem l'shalom malakhei
ha-shalom malakhei Elyon
mi-Melekh Malkhei
ha-Melakhim
Ha-Kadosh barukh Hu.

Barkhuni l'shalom malakhei
ha-shalom malakhei Elyon
mi-Melekh Malkhei
ha-Melakhim
Ha-Kadosh barukh Hu.

Tzeitkhem l'shalom
malakhei ha-shalom
malakhei Elyon
mi-Melekh Malkhei
ha-Melakhim
Ha-Kadosh barukh Hu.

Shalom to you Messengers, Angels of the Most High,
Angels of the Ruler, the Ruler of Rulers,
The Holy One who is to be Praised.

Come in Peace,
Angels of Peace,
Angels of the Most High
Angels of the Ruler, the Ruler of Rulers,
The Holy One who is to be Praised.

Bless me with Peace,
Angels of Peace,
Angels of the Most High
Angels of the Ruler, the Ruler of Rulers,
The Holy One who is to be Praised.

Go in Peace,
Angels of Peace,
Angels of the Most High
Angels of the Ruler, the Ruler of Rulers,
The Holy One who is to be Praised.

4
Blessing of the Children

1. Place hands on child's head
2. Say the appropriate blessing (sons or daughters)
3. Add your own wishes and thoughts
4. Say the "Priestly Blessing for all children).
5. Hug, kiss, etc.

For Sons

יְשִׂימְךָ אֱלֹהִים
כְּאֶפְרַיִם וְכִמְנַשֶּׁה.

Y'simkha Elohim k'Efrayim v'khiMenashe

For Daughters

יְשִׂימֵךְ אֱלֹהִים
כְּשָׂרָה רִבְקָה רָחֵל וְלֵאָה.

Y'simeikh Elohim k'Sarah, Rivka, Rahel, v'Leah.

For All Children

יְבָרֶכְךָ יהוה וְיִשְׁמְרֶךָ
יָאֵר יהוה פָּנָיו אֵלֶיךָ וִיחֻנֶּךָּ
יִשָּׂא יהוה פָּנָיו אֵלֶיךָ
וְיָשֵׂם לְךָ שָׁלוֹם.

Y'varekh'kha Adonai v'yishm'rekha.
Ya'er Adonai panav elekha vihunekha.
Yisa Adonai panav elekha v'yasem l'kha shalom.

May Adonai bless you and guard you.
May Adonai shine the Divine light upon you and be good to you.
May Adonai face you and give you peace.

5
Kiddush

1. You may stand or sit.
2. Lift the Kiddush cup.
3. Say or sing these brakhot.
4. Everyone may join in starting at *"Ki vanu..."*
5. Drink the wine.

בָּרוּךְ אַתָּה יהוה אֱלֹהֵינוּ מֶלֶךְ הָעוֹלָם בּוֹרֵא פְּרִי הַגָּפֶן.

בָּרוּךְ אַתָּה יהוה אֱלֹהֵינוּ מֶלֶךְ הָעוֹלָם אֲשֶׁר קִדְּשָׁנוּ בְּמִצְוֹתָיו וְרָצָה בָנוּ. וְשַׁבַּת קָדְשׁוֹ בְּאַהֲבָה וּבְרָצוֹן הִנְחִילָנוּ. זִכָּרוֹן לְמַעֲשֵׂה בְרֵאשִׁית. כִּי הוּא יוֹם תְּחִלָּה לְמִקְרָאֵי קֹדֶשׁ זֵכֶר לִיצִיאַת מִצְרָיִם. כִּי בָנוּ בָחַרְתָּ וְאוֹתָנוּ קִדַּשְׁתָּ מִכָּל הָעַמִּים. וְשַׁבַּת קָדְשְׁךָ בְּאַהֲבָה וּבְרָצוֹן הִנְחַלְתָּנוּ. בָּרוּךְ אַתָּה יהוה מְקַדֵּשׁ הַשַּׁבָּת.

Barukh atah Adonai Eloheinu melekh ha-olam borei p'ri ha-gafen.
Barukh atah Adonai Eloheinu melekh ha-olam
asher kidshanu b'mitzvotav v'ratza vanu
V'Shabbat kodsho b'ahava u-v'ratzon hinhilanu—
zikaron l'ma'asei v'reishit.
Ki hu yom t'hilah l'mikra'ei kodesh—
zekher litziyat Mitzrayim.
Ki vanu vaharta v'otanu kidashta mikol ha-amim;
v'Shabbat kodsh'kha b'ahava u-v'ratzon hinhaltanu.
Barukh atah Adonai M'kadesh ha-Shabbat.
Praised are You, Adonai, our God, Ruler of the Cosmos, the One Who creates the fruit of the vine.

Praised are You, Adonai, our God, Ruler of the Cosmos, Who made us holy through the mitzvot and Who is pleased with us. And the One Who gave us the holy Shabbat, with love and satisfaction, as a rememberance of the work of creation. And, as a remembrance of the Exodus from Egypt—making it first among the holy days when we gather. For You chose us from among all people and made us holy, and gave us as an inheritance Your holy Shabbat with love and satisfaction. Praised are You, Adonai, the One Who makes Shabbat Holy.

6
Washing Hands

1. Fill a cup or pitcher with water.
2. Pour over both hands.
3. Lift hands.
4. Say the brakhah.
5. Dry hands.

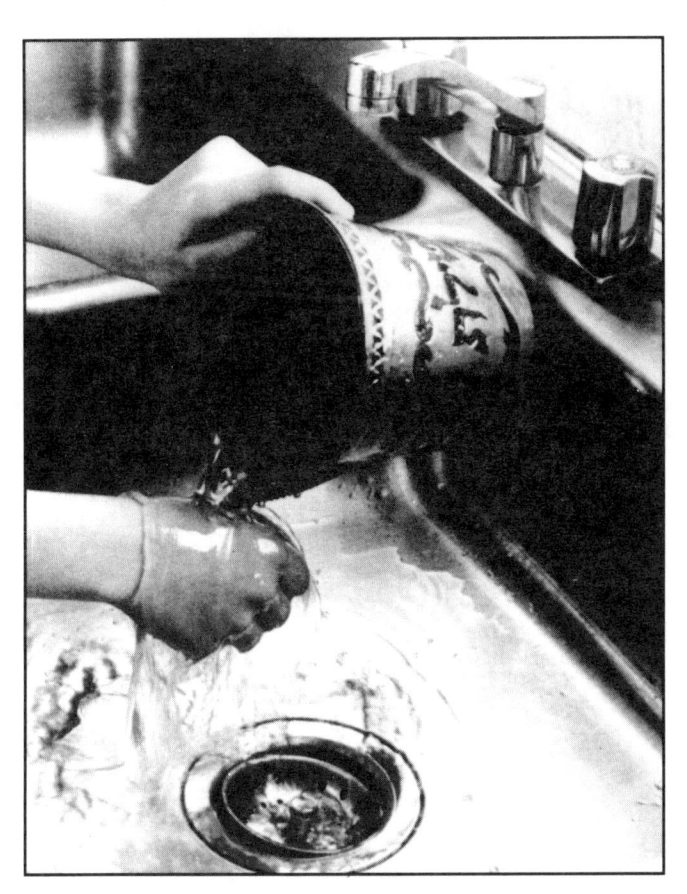

בָּרוּךְ אַתָּה יהוה
אֱלֹהֵינוּ מֶלֶךְ הָעוֹלָם
אֲשֶׁר קִדְּשָׁנוּ בְּמִצְוֹתָיו
וְצִוָּנוּ עַל נְטִילַת יָדָיִם.

Barukh atah Adonai Eloheinu melekh ha-olam asher kidshanu b'mitzvotav v'tzivanu al netilat yadayim.

Praised are You, Adonai, our God, Ruler of the Cosmos, who made us holy through the mitzvot and made it a mitzvah for us to lift up (and wash) our hands.

7
Ha-Motzi

1. Uncover the Hallot.
2. Nick the chosen Hallah with a knife.
3. Say the brakhah.
4. Tear or slice off a piece of the bread.
5. Sprinkle with salt.
6. Eat

בָּרוּךְ אַתָּה יהוה
אֱלֹהֵינוּ מֶלֶךְ הָעוֹלָם
הַמּוֹצִיא לֶחֶם מִן הָאָרֶץ.

Barukh atah Adonai Eloheinu melekh ha-olam ha-motzi lehem min ha-aretz.

Praised are You, Adonai, our God, Ruler of the Cosmos, the One Who brings forth bread from the earth.

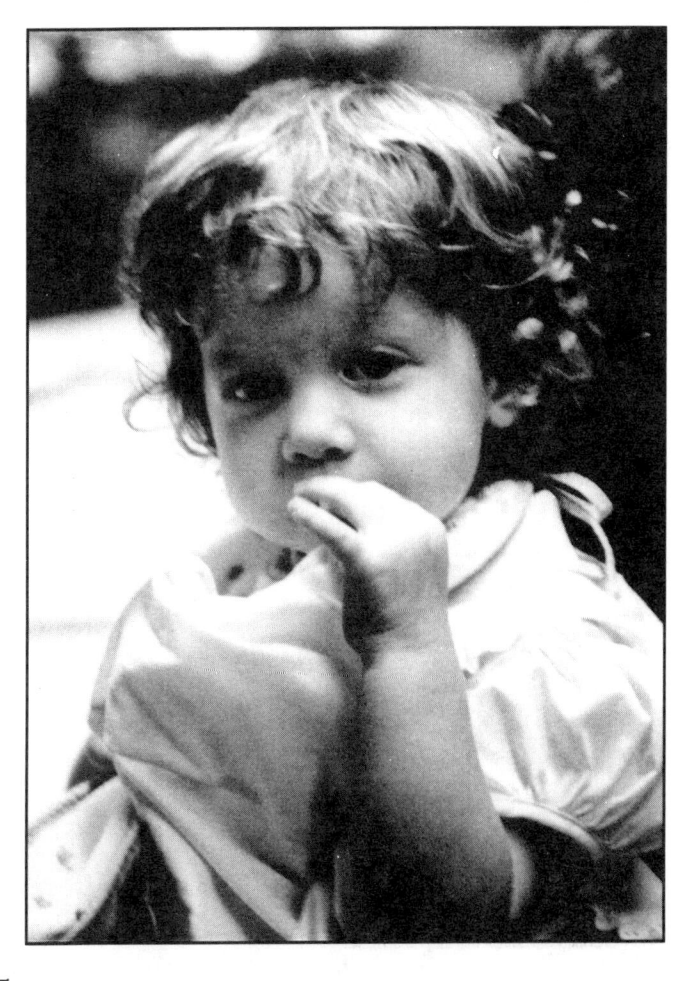

8
Birkat Ha-Mazon

1. Finish eating.
2. Clear the table. Remove or cover all knives.
3. Sing or say Birkat Ha-Mazon. (This is a very abridged version.) If Birkat Ha-Mazon is very new to you, you may only want to say the last line.

בָּרוּךְ אַתָּה יהוה
אֱלֹהֵינוּ מֶלֶךְ הָעוֹלָם
הַזָּן אֶת הָעוֹלָם כֻּלּוֹ בְּטוּבוֹ
בְּחֵן בְּחֶסֶד וּבְרַחֲמִים.
הוּא נוֹתֵן לֶחֶם לְכָל בָּשָׂר
כִּי לְעוֹלָם חַסְדּוֹ
וּבְטוּבוֹ הַגָּדוֹל
תָּמִיד לֹא חָסַר לָנוּ
וְאַל יֶחְסַר לָנוּ
מָזוֹן לְעוֹלָם וָעֶד
בַּעֲבוּר שְׁמוֹ הַגָּדוֹל.
כִּי הוּא אֵל זָן וּמְפַרְנֵס לַכֹּל
וּמֵטִיב לַכֹּל וּמֵכִין מָזוֹן
לְכָל בְּרִיּוֹתָיו אֲשֶׁר בָּרָא.

בָּרוּךְ אַתָּה יהוה
הַזָּן אֶת הַכֹּל.

Barukh atah Adonai
Eloheinu melekh ha-olam
Hazan et ha-olam kulo
b'tuvo b'hen b'hesed
u-v'rahamim.
Hu noten lehem l'khol
basar ki l'olam hasdo.
U'v'tuvo ha-gadol tamid lo
hasar lanu
v'al yehsar lanu mazon
l'olam va'ed ba'avur sh'mo
ha-gadol.
Ki hu El zan u-m'farnes
la-kol,
u-metiv la-kol, u-mekhin
mazon l'khol b'riyotav asher
bara.

Barukh atah Adonai Hazan et ha-kol.

Praised are You, Adonai, Our God, Ruler of the Cosmos, the One Who feeds the world, all of it, with goodness, with graciousness, with love and with compassion. The One Who provides food to every creature because of everlasting Divine love. God's great goodness has never failed us, and will never fail to feed us, for the sake of God's great name. Because God is the One Who feeds all, and does good for all, and prepares food for all creatures which God created.

Praised are You Adonai, the One Who feeds all.

Havdalah Service

Assemble a full cup of wine, a lighted havdalah candle and the spice box on table or tray.

1
Wine

1. Lift cup.
2. Say brakhah.
3. Do not drink the wine.

בָּרוּךְ אַתָּה יהוה
אֱלֹהֵינוּ מֶלֶךְ הָעוֹלָם
בּוֹרֵא פְּרִי הַגָּפֶן.

Barukh atah Adonai Eloheinu melekh ha-olam borei p'ri ha-gafen.
Praised are You, Adonai, our God, Ruler of the Cosmos, the One Who creates the fruit of the vine.

2
Smell

1. Lift spice box.
2. Say brakhah.
3. Have everyone smell the spices.

בָּרוּךְ אַתָּה יהוה
אֱלֹהֵינוּ מֶלֶךְ הָעוֹלָם
בּוֹרֵא מִינֵי בְשָׂמִים.

Barukh atah Adonai Eloheinu melekh ha-olam borei mi'nei besamim.
Praised are You, Adonai, our God, Ruler of the Cosmos, the One Who creates all kinds of spices.

3
Fire

1. Say the following brakhah.
2. Catch the reflection of the flames of the havdalah candle in your fingernails.

בָּרוּךְ אַתָּה יהוה
אֱלֹהֵינוּ מֶלֶךְ הָעוֹלָם
בּוֹרֵא מְאוֹרֵי הָאֵשׁ.

Barukh atah Adonai Eloheinu melekh ha-olam borei m'orei ha-esh.
Praised are You, Adonai, our God, Ruler of the Cosmos, the One Who creates the lights of fire.

4
Separation

1. Lift the cup of wine again.
2. Say this brakhah.
3. Drink some of the wine.
4. Extinguish the candle in the remainder of the wine.
5. Hug, kiss, and wish each other Shavuah Tov (A Good Week).

בָּרוּךְ אַתָּה יהוה
אֱלֹהֵינוּ מֶלֶךְ הָעוֹלָם
הַמַּבְדִּיל בֵּין קֹדֶשׁ לְחוֹל
בֵּין אוֹר לְחֹשֶׁךְ
בֵּן יִשְׂרָאֵל לָעַמִּים
בֵּין יוֹם הַשְּׁבִיעִי
לְשֵׁשֶׁת יְמֵי הַמַּעֲשֶׂה
בָּרוּךְ אַתָּה יהוה
הַמַּבְדִּיל בֵּין קֹדֶשׁ לְחוֹל.

Barukh atah Adonai Eloheinu melekh ha-olam
Ha-Mavdil bein kodesh l'hol
bein or l'hoshekh
bein Yisrael la'amim,
bein Yom ha-Sh'vi-i l'shei-shet y'mei ha-ma-aseh
Barukh atah Adonai, Ha-Mavdil bein kodesh l'hol.
Praised are You, Adonai, Our God, Ruler of the cosmos, the One Who distinguishes between the holy and the ordinary: between light and dark, between Israel and other peoples, between the Seventh Day and the six days of work. Praised are You, Adonai, the One Who separates the holy and the ordinary.